Mommy I'm ALIVE

The Miracle of Baby Ozzy

by
Janice A. Lee

© 2023 Mommy I'm Alive - The Miracle of Baby Ozzy

All rights reserved. No part of this publication may be reproduced, stored in a retrieval system, or transmitted in any form or by any means – for example, electronic, mechanical, photocopying, recording or any other – except for brief quotations in printed reviews – without the prior written permission of the publishers or author in accordance with the provisions of the Copyright, Designs and Patents Acts 1988.

Unless otherwise stated Scriptures are taken from the King James Version (KJV) and the New International Version®, NIV® Copyright ©1973, 1978, 1984, 2011 by Biblica, Inc.® Used by permission. All rights reserved worldwide.

This represents the experiences of Janice A. Lee. Any resemblance of character(s) and situation(s) to real-life character(s) and situation(s) are strictly coincidental.

Published by SelectArrow Ltd. www.selectarrow.net
Email: office.selectarrow@gmail.com

ISBN: 978-1-7398830-2-7

Cover and interior design: Homer Slack
Editor: Angela Slack

Dedication

This book is dedicated to my three wonderful grandsons, Finn, Liam and Ozzy. As you journey here on earth you will be faced with life's many challenges, however my prayer is that you may all come to know my Lord and Saviour, Jesus Christ; He gives peace to the weary and strength to those that are downcast. He is the giver and sustainer of life and to know Him is to have life everlasting.

Psalms 89:1 AMP

"I will sing of the goodness and lovingkindness of the LORD forever; With my mouth I will make known Your faithfulness from generation to generation."

Acknowledgement

The manifestation of this book would not be possible without the support and encouragement of my family and friends. Firstly, I am especially thankful to Zack, my son-in-law and Suzanna my daughter, who gave me permission to write part of their amazing story. I love you guys and your steadfastness in holding on to God's promise, it is a testimony of what God can do when we trust in His word. Thank you also for writing the foreword for this book.

To my husband Chris, who is my front row cheerleader, my heartfelt gratitude. My dear sisters Claudette and Joey and their husbands Pastor Horace Forbes and Arthur Hamilton. I can always depend on you to cheer me on and pray me up. To my many cousins near and far, you guys stood with us during those difficult weeks and months and encamped around us like the wall of Jericho, thanks so much for your prayers, love, support and encouragement.

I am grateful to my church community at Swallowfield Chapel, especially the ladies in connect group-*Expression of Christ*; you guys will never understand how deeply I appreciate you all. Thanks also to my own connect couples' group and my POPs-*People of Praise*. I truly appreciate and love every one of you.

Thanks to Dayna, Frances and Dacia, my prayer partners, who held my arms up when I was too weak to hold them up myself. Thank you Frances for your endorsement. Thanks to Major Richard and Dr.

Claudette Cooke for your prayers and endorsement. Thanks also to Dr Roan Paul Earle for his love and encouragement and for his endorsement of this book.

To my publishers and editors Homer and Angela Slack who worked tirelessly in bringing the dream of this book into reality. From the first moment you read the manuscript you embraced my vision and this is the result. Thank you Homer for your creative design of the book cover and the complete layout of the book. Angela, thank you for your guidance and encouragement. When I looked back at the first draft I sent you and how you have beautifully assisted me in crafting my thoughts into a lovely story, I am truly grateful.

Last but not least, I thank my Lord for giving me the opportunity to testify of His faithfulness, goodness, mercy and grace and for allowing me to place on record this marvellous miracle.

"Understand, therefore, that the Lord your God is indeed God. He is the faithful God who keeps his covenant for a thousand generations and lavishes his unfailing love on those who love him and obey his commands." Deuteronomy 7:9 NLT

Endorsement

The story you are about to read is an incredible story of God's grace. Janice A. Lee's *Mommy, I am Alive*, will build your faith for a moment when you or a loved one will need it most. It resonates with all of us that have faced crises and desperately needed God to come through.

Janice, tells the story of her grandson, Ozzy, a miracle baby. At 17 weeks' gestation, his mother's water broke, and she was given the prognosis that her pregnancy was not viable. At 29 weeks, Ozzy was born by C-section by a medically verifiable miracle.

I was honoured to be at Zack and Suzie's wedding. She is always dear to me, and so I was overjoyed when a few months later she said that she was pregnant. They decided to wait until the end of the first trimester to announce the pregnancy. It was about a week after her official announcement, Suzanna called me with the frightening news. We cried and prayed and asked the Lord for direction.

Getting pregnant was a miracle for Suzie and now she needed a super miracle. I bear witness to the unfolding miracle of Ozzy, the remarkable tenacity of Suzie's faith in the midst of legitimate fears. Together, Suzie and Zack kept believing as they lived through these months, caring for each other, their older son, and working with their medical team to bring Ozzy into the world. Thank God, they were not alone. They had a God believing family supporting them and prayer warriors all over the world praying daily for Ozzy. In particular, Janice was a daily voice of hope, and an emotional pillow that they could rest on, and she gives us a perspective on the miracle that no one else can.

Janice tells the story with authentic emotional and spiritual transparency. It is Ozzy's, Suzie's and Zack's story and now Janice has brought us in and it's our story.

In crises, it is faith in God and the support of loved ones that are our pillars of wisdom, resilience and hope. Janice invites us into the heart of the journey as a grandma and mom and this book *Mommy, I am Alive*, is a divinely inspired message of God's perspective on life, it's challenges and God's grace to triumph. You will be touched and blessed as you read.

"Uncle Ro"
Roan Paul Earle
Grateful Uncle of Suzanna
Apple Valley,
California, USA.

Endorsement

When our niece Suzanna and her husband Zack tearfully decided that they would not end their pregnancy, despite the advice by her doctors, we set out on an emotional "roller-coaster" with them along with other family members. At 17 weeks into the pregnancy, Suzie's Amniotic Sac was compromised and the fluid was leaking out.

The doctors presented a compelling outlook that the pregnancy would not end well, citing the onset of infection, miscarriage and irreparable harm compromising future pregnancy opportunities and the prognosis stirred anxiety in all of us.

Learning to stand with our adult children in support rather than to provide advice, we decided to pray and stay in faith with Suzie and Zack. All this was the start of a journey into the unknown of medicine, nutrition and faith.

Confoundedly, Ozzy was in darkness, as the technology of Ultrasound requires fluid to 'see' so that doctors would be able to properly assess what was happening. What adamantly existed was a very strong heartbeat, which signified that Ozzy was there, where he should be, we just could not see him.

Suzie and Zack did their part, they prayed, Suzie kept as still as she could, carrying out her job functions from her bed, conducting interviews and sourcing new talents for her company, and she drank lots of bone broth. As shared, our education in this field was all new.

There was one day in particular where the report was not good as no pockets of fluid were seen and as we drove them home and they cried, we prayed out loud for God's continued mercy and peace upon them.

This journey was not an easy one for anyone involved as like Ozzy, we were in the dark, walking by faith, not by sight. Each day we prayed for enough faith to trust and believe even as we held our breaths.

Ozzy is a miracle, there is no doubt about that. As tiny as he was when he was delivered at 29 weeks old, he was called the 'Rock Star' by doctors and nurses at the UCLA hospital who attended to him or visited just to see how things were developing. Was it easy to get to the end? Not for his parents, his grandmother and those of us who were praying. However, God ordained this miracle and God is sovereign.

We endorse that every word is true as the story is shared. Join us as we give all praise and thanks to God for what He has done!

Mr and Mrs Arthur and Joan Hamilton
Uncle and Aunt
St. Andrew, Jamaica,
West Indies.

Endorsement

Every now and then, one gets to participate in a mighty move of God that reminds us that He is still the God of miracles. The God who hears, cares, and responds to the heart cry of His children. This book, *Mommy I Am Alive*, is about the unwavering faith of an ordinary family against formidable odds.

Richard and I are privileged to be a part of the ongoing miracle that characterises the life of Ozzy and his beloved family. We remember when Janice called to say that Suzie and Zack were pregnant. Pregnant with joy, hope and gratitude to God for the gift of life in Suzie's womb. We rejoiced at the great news and prayed for their baby's safe development. Janice kept me (Claudette) up to date on the progress of their pregnancy and the well-being of Suzie, Zack and their older child, Finn. All were doing well. We Rejoiced.

Then, the fateful call from Janice came, saying, "All is not well with baby Ozzy." We went into warfare prayer, petitioning God to preserve his life. Words of encouragement filled our WhatsApp chats. We declared the word of God that says, despite what seemed impossible, all things were possible with God. We believed that God would get the glory in the outcome.

We joined the family in refusing to accept the dismal outcome that was 'prophesied' by some doctors for Ozzy. Disregarding the prognosis of Science, they believed firmly in the Word of God, continuously giving thanks for His miracle-working power in this precious baby's life.

I read to Richard the message Janice sent me. He and I had not too long before prayed for Ozzy. It read, "Suzie had an emergency C-section this morning. She is resting. Ozzy came out with a fist up and crying. They said, 'He is looking good. Praise the Lord!'"

We rejoiced. God had been faithful! Against all odds, Ozzy is here. Ozzy, the cutest, sweetest little boy, is growing in the nurture and love of his family and the divine protection of the Lord. Richard and I continue to pray for Ozzy and to declare that Ozzy "… will not die but live, and proclaim what the Lord has done." Psalm 118:17.

We wholeheartedly endorse this retelling of Ozzy's Journey, *Mommy I Am Alive*, through Janice's eyes and pray that it will nurture your faith to believe in the God of miracles.

Major Richard Cooke -Founder and President Joy Town Community Development Foundation and Elder, Covenant City Church

Dr. Claudette Cooke - Founder and Convener of Signature Woman Ministry and Executive Director Jamaica Broilers Group Foundations.
St. Andrew,
Jamaica, West Indies.

Endorsement

I am honoured to endorse this incredible book, *Mommy I Am Alive*, written by a Christian grandmother and prayer warrior who has experienced a miraculous and inspiring journey. Janice A. Lee's, unwavering faith and remarkable love for her daughter and unborn grandchild is truly awe-inspiring.

In the face of immense challenges, when her daughter was told to abort her baby due to health issues, this grandmother stood firm in her belief in the power of prayer and the goodness of God. Despite the doubts and uncertainties surrounding them, she continued to trust in God's plan and His ability to work miracles.

The journey chronicled in this book is nothing short of extraordinary. It is a testament to the strength of a mother's love and the unwavering faith that can move mountains. Through every obstacle and setback, this family relied on their belief in God's sovereignty and the power of prayer to carry them through.

What sets this book apart is not only the remarkable story it tells but also the author's obedience to the leading of the Holy Spirit. To document this journey and share it as a testimony and source of encouragement for others is a selfless act of love and devotion.

The words contained within these pages will undoubtedly touch the hearts and souls of all who read them. They remind us that God indeed answers prayer and performs miracles in our lives. They serve as a powerful reminder that even in our darkest moments, we can find hope and strength in our faith.

I highly recommend *Mommy I Am Alive*, to anyone in need of inspiration, encouragement, and a reminder of the incredible power of prayer. May it bring comfort to those facing similar challenges and ignite a renewed sense of faith in the hearts of all who read it.

Frances Yeo
Friend and Prayer Partner
Prayer Ministry Leader,
Swallowfield Chapel,
Kingston, Jamaica.

Endorsement

Mummy I'm Alive, is a beautiful account of the anguish, hope and joy a family experiences when faced with the possibility of an extremely pre-term birth. Janice A. Lee, describes the long and difficult journey traveled by baby Ozzy and his family and gives us insight into the complexities of the decisions encountered along the way.

As a tiny preemie in the NICU, baby Ozzy faced many challenges to survival and required the concerted efforts of a team of doctors, nurses, respiratory therapists, pharmacists, physical therapists and dietitians in order to survive the first days and weeks of his life. Throughout the book, the author invites us to share the joy of each wonderful moment in Ozzy's progress.

It was a privilege for me to have played a role in supporting baby Ozzy through those critical early stages in the NICU and to watch him as he took his tiny but monumental steps towards healing and growth.

Mummy I'm Alive, is a testament to the resilience and strength of baby Ozzy and will undoubtedly be an inspiration for others facing similar challenges.

Catherine Ekwa-Ekoko, MD, Neonatologist
Los Angeles,
California, USA.

Contents

Chapter	Page
1. We Are Having A Baby!	2
2. The Big Decision	10
3. The Consultation	18
4. Five Long Weeks In The Hospital	24
5. Prayer and More Prayer	30
6. Labour of Love	34
7. Trusting And Giving Thanks	38
8. Miracles Do Happen	44
9. To God Be The Glory!	50
10. Photo Album	52

Foreword

You can never prepare yourself to hear the words "This pregnancy is over, you should try again," from a well-respected Maternal-Fetal Medicine Specialist when you're 17 weeks pregnant. We wanted to reject the assessment but the science said otherwise. When we told Janice (affectionately called 'Gramma Jamaica' in our household) what the doctors said, she immediately rejected the death sentence our baby was given.

In true form, Janice jumped into action and formed a network of prayer warriors, believers, and intercessors to petition the gates of heaven for Ozzy's life. She has always been a pillar of faithfulness and her life of abundance reflects this. She is an esteemed global businesswoman, teacher, mentor, author, exceptional wife, mother, sister and friend.

We can honestly say that Ozzy is alive because of the faith of our parents. They have passed on a legacy of grace to us, their children, and their grandchildren. Gramma Jamaica, from day one, championed the belief that despite the odds Ozzy would survive. If she had doubts or uncertainties she never let us see them. When she spoke with us, she consistently touted the message of faith for the seemingly impossible.

Over the years, Janice's example to our family as a devout disciple of Christ has inspired our faith, in some ways saved our marriage, and without a doubt played a crucial role in our ability to withstand the treacherous journey of a high-risk pregnancy, the birth of a micro-preemie and ninety days stay in the NICU. We are blessed to have her and honoured that she would share this story through her eyes and unique perspective.

Be prepared for an emotional rollercoaster, one filled with moments of despair and hope, suspense, and relief at God's faithfulness. As you read we encourage you to reflect on times in your own life where God has shown up in miraculous ways. Perhaps you are in need of a miracle in your life right now. Let Ozzy's story and Janice's testimony of faith inspire you to believe in miracles.

Ozzy is a daily reminder to our family to choose faith over fear. Though we would never wish to repeat this experience, nor would we wish it on another family, we are grateful to have gone through it, as it has strengthened our faith and solidified our family bond. Ozzy's life is a continuous testimony, one Gramma Jamaica stays extremely close to. Ozzy knows her face and her voice, from his very first week of life she was by his side; singing, praying, believing for our little miracle. Every day his smile reminds us of God's love and mercy, may this story be a reminder to you as well.

Mr and Mrs Zachary and Suzanna Duthie-Mack
Thankful parents of Ozzy.
Los Angeles,
California,
USA.

Preface

In Matthew 17:20, Jesus answering His disciples said, *"Because of your unbelief; for assuredly, I say to you, if you have faith as a mustard seed, you will say to this mountain, 'Move from here to there,' and it will move, and nothing will be impossible for you."*

The ring of my mobile phone at 6 a.m. on the morning of July 2, 2022, jolted me so much that I literally jumped out of bed. Now standing, dazed, I paused in mid-air, running my fingers through my hair, brushing it away from my face. Making my way stealthily, phone in hand, towards my dressing room.

I looked at the clock on the counter. I looked across the room at my husband still sleeping in the bed and wondered if he heard the ring. His soft snore and the fact that he did not budge made me realise he didn't. The room was dark except for the light coming from the dressing room where I stood. As usual, I felt very cold in this house because my nephew in the other room likes the house very cold as he said the air does not reach his room as it should.

My mind was thinking many things all at once and I prayed that it was not her, but it was her. She lives over 2,700 miles away and it was 3 a.m. at her location.

With bated breath I answered the phone, my heart beating so fast I felt as if it was coming through my mouth! I heard her say, "Mommy, I think I am going into labour." I felt weak and my mind screamed: *This cannot be, it's too soon! Will the baby survive? What will his physical and mental development be like?* Despite my fears, I tried to remain calm while my head was having its own conversation.

He will be alright, think positively, don't panic Janice, don't let her hear any panic in your voice, speak reassuringly to her, she needs you now more than ever. Janice, get a grip! Suzie needs you. Okay, PHEEEEEW! I slowly exhaled breaking the hanging silence.

I will handle this, I am a mother, after all, I can do this. God help me!

I felt like I was having an out-of-body experience where I knew that something was happening but I was so numb that I was not fully connected to the scene. This, was my mental state that morning. It felt unreal.

She was in the hospital for the last five weeks and doing great. We were all hopeful that the baby would not arrive until about 34 weeks. However, at this time he was just at 29 weeks gestation, in the breach position, and with many uncertainties about his development. There was therefore great cause for concern.

Based on the science he should not have even reached this far. In fact, the doctors were very negative when the couple decided not to terminate the pregnancy. I prayed with her that morning and tried to calm her and reassure her that God was in control. Nevertheless, my mind was having a different conversation, *Please Lord not now, he needs a few more weeks, I am not sure he will survive at this stage.*

The morning it happened I was on my way to the airport and I proceeded as planned. I believe I was hoping that she would call back and say that everything was okay and it was a false alarm. However, at about 8:30 am, as I was heading towards the departure gate to board my flight, my mobile phone rang again and I heard her say in a calm voice, "I am being prepared for an emergency cesarean section.".Again, the weakness came upon me but in a greater force this time. My knees seemed like they were going to let me down and without even realising it, I had stopped walking.

I looked around at the people who were rushing, rushing and I wondered, *Why do they seem so normal while I was feeling the earth moving beneath my feet?* Everything seemed so calm and normal as airports should be. I heard voices which appeared distant, even though I knew the owners of those voices were right beside me. I inhaled the early morning smells of coffee, toast and some other aromas that I could not recognise. I heard a child complaining and a mother saying "Hurry or we may miss the flight.' My mind was ordering me to run but my feet refused to move, while having the same mental conversation, *No, not now, he is only at 29 weeks gestation! It is too soon, and what about her, will she be alright?*

The doctors had told her that they would have to do a major cut because he was so tiny. I could hear a distant voice in my head, saying, *Keep calm, keep calm, and don't panic.*

I am at a loss. I stopped walking and thought, *Should I turn back?* Turning back towards the security checkpoint may not be a good idea since they would not allow me through that way. Since I could not go back, I turned towards the gate to board my flight. I felt like a zombie. *Am I going crazy?* I talked to myself. I have never felt so lost, I was totally confused about what to do or where to turn. *So, this is how it feels when one is completely lost?* I heard the distant voices again, *Keep calm, start walking, and get a hold of yourself.* I felt as if someone was guiding me and whispering these calming words in my ears.

I called my husband and asked him, "Should I just find a flight to Los Angeles or should I continue to Jamaica?" All the time my mind was in a fog, I tried to retrieve my bag from the aeroplane but it was not that simple. Looking back, I realised that fear and anxiety are crippling forces. I am not an individual who is usually indecisive or even uncertain about the next step. However, that morning, I could not figure out what to do. I called my sister, and she told me to stop thinking and just take the next available flight to Los Angeles, which I did. I felt like a child who needed to be told what to do.

While waiting for my suitcase to be taken off the flight, I found a seat in the baggage area and I sat down and just began to cry shamelessly. While I cried, I reflected on the last three months of waiting for this very moment but praying and hoping that instead of 29 weeks delivery, it would be 34 weeks. "God, please help Suzie and the baby to be safe and healthy, I prayed silently."

Introduction

"Lo, children are a heritage of the LORD: and the fruit of the womb is His reward" (Psalms 127:3).

The first time I saw him I cried, my heart was bursting with joy, I was standing but my spirit was dancing for joy, rejoicing in what God had done. I looked down at this tiny little creation and thought, *This is what a miracle looks and feels like.* After four months of praying, I was certain that God was hearing me but I was apprehensive about the desired outcome. Four months of standing on the word of God that, "If we believe, all things are possible." When Ozzy was two weeks old they allowed me to hold him and he looked intently at me, I was in awe. I asked the nurse if he could see me and she said, he only saw slight images but he recognised my voice. Each day I visited, I was amazed that he not only recognised my voice but his favourite nurse as he could look in the direction of her voice whenever she was close by.

I have always believed that life is a miracle, however, when the odds are not looking so good in the natural world, it becomes God's supernatural intervention.

God breathed His breath into His magnificent creation and called him man, and He said it was good. He then created a companion for the first man, a woman, and said, "It was very good," woman. They dwelt with their Creator and had sweet fellowship, then one day the Creator called, "Adam where are you?" The man timidly replied that he was hiding because he felt afraid.

The couple's eyes were opened and they became conscious of their nakedness.

Since that time when our human fore-parents sinned against God, the human race has lived in fear of the judgement of God and shame. Sin, which leads to death (separation from God) leads to spiralling downwards into a vacuum of fear and insecurity about life and our place in this world. Is this the end? The giver and sustainer of life knew that this would happen, so He unfolded His master plan to restore fellowship with His precious creation, His pride and joy, humanity.

"For God so loved the world that he gave his only begotten son that whoever believes in Him should have everlasting life". John 3:16, NKJV

"But he was pierced for our transgressions, he was crushed for our iniquities; the punishment that brought us peace was on him, and by his wounds we are healed". Isaiah 53: 5, NIV

This memoir is about the love of God and how taking God at His word can move mountains if you allow Him to be your guide.

Each life is a precious gift from God, we can choose to embrace that gift or we can abuse the gift. The one who gives life is the same one who preserves and sustains life.

I am compelled to share this miracle story because many mothers, expectant mothers, or grandmothers may have experienced or are experiencing similar situations. What do you do when the report about your baby is not good? When you are told that the precious gift growing inside of you may not survive? Or if he does, he will be faced with many physical and mental issues? Where can you turn?

There are no guarantees in life, except death, this is the only certainty, that we all must die. However, for those of us who believe in Jesus Christ, it's the gateway to eternal life with our Lord, it is not the end. I believe that while we are here on earth there is a God who cares about all that concerns us and He is always desirous to shower us with unspeakable blessings.

My grandson Ozzy, challenged the odds, he is a strong and determined little man, it's as if he knew that if he was determined to live, God was able and willing to work the miracle. This is the reason why I am sharing Ozzy's story; the miracle of baby Ozzy is documented in the hospital records forever. *Mommy I Am Alive,* chronicles the journey of a couple who despite the odds trusted a God who promised that, no matter what the situation, He would never leave us or forsake us. (Hebrews 13:5) The book shares the pain, sorrow and joy of what it means to have faith even when the report is not good.

My prayer is that no matter your situation, no matter the reports from the doctors, you too will allow God to work in your situation. The outcome may not always be the desired outcome but I believe that whatever the outcome, God is sovereign and in absolute control! May blessings remain with you as you embark on your expectant journey,

Janice

Mommy I Am Alive

.1

Chapter 1

We Are Having A Baby!

In late January 2022, my daughter who had just got married in early December called me excitedly to tell me that she was pregnant. We were thrilled as, based on statistics, once a woman passes a certain age it becomes more difficult to conceive. In fact, it is said that fertility starts declining at age 30 and faster after 35. She was 38 years old. We were elated and happy for her and her husband. This would be our third grandchild as my daughter has a stepson and our son's wife gave birth to a boy in 2021.

I would like to think of myself as a 'Glama' because I have never really seen myself as a traditional grandmother type. I am that sixty-something-year-old woman you meet at a restaurant, party or on the street and you wonder aloud about her age. I have often been told that I am a 'dresser' and I love to dress up.

However, meeting Finn, our daughter's stepson changed me, the moment he said, "Hi Grandma". Finn, is a bundle of energy, a joy to be around, very observant, full of talk, and pranks and can hold a conversation like an adult even at 5 years old. Then in December of 2019, we met Liam, our son's son, though only nine months old at the time he was full of life and very busy. He wore out his grandpa and I, always wanting to walk even though he could not at that time. We are proud of our growing family and excited for an addition. All we asked for was a healthy little one. Both of our children are in their thirties and both live on two different continents, therefore we do not see them very often.

Before I became a grandparent, I often heard people with grandchildren talk about them with joy. In fact, someone told me a few years ago that once you become a grandparent you have found the real purpose of life. It's amazing how you love your children deeply but once you are introduced to your grandchildren your heart can expand beyond your greatest imagination.

I was thrilled that I would be a 'Glama' again and when Suzie went to the doctor to confirm her pregnancy and get her due date, we discussed that I would spend some time with her once the baby arrived. A few weeks later, we received the call that the baby was a boy. To me, it didn't matter if the baby was a boy or girl because all I prayed for was a healthy child.

In March, I visited Suzie and Zack in California. Santa Barbara is a small place by American standards, with beautiful beaches, and the perfect climate and even though an expensive place, it is ideal for raising a family. However, despite the beauty of the place I once more wondered why they had moved so far away from us. I live in Jamaica and California seemed like another world away from us. The fact is, they love living in California. That's where Zack was born and raised. His parents live there and both Suzie and Zack met while on their way there a few years ago. They love the beach and the laid-back culture of Santa Barbara. Suzie would often say it reminds her of Jamaica in terms of its size, the flowers and the beaches. She would often say, "It's an island feel in a first-world country." The three weeks I spent was great as I was able to bond with Finn and give support to Suzie who was having a bit of morning sickness.

One day Suzie asked me what I thought about the name Ozzy for the baby. At the time I thought that Ozzy was the shortened version of Oswald and to me, it sounded like an old English name. However, they explained that the name Ozzy means "strength of God." To be honest, I was not too excited about this name and I told them so. I left Santa Barbara in the early part of April assuring Suzie that I would visit again in September when the baby was due.

4.

17 Weeks - Fetus Not Viable!

About a week after returning from California I received a call from Suzie. Her voice was very shaky as one in deep distress. She told me that it appeared that her amniotic sac broke and she was on her way to the emergency centre. I was devastated as I knew the implication of what this would mean. The news was not good when she went to the hospital. The doctor told her there was no amniotic fluid in the sac and the baby would not survive. He told her that the best option was to terminate the pregnancy immediately. They said the baby was not viable at this stage (meaning he could not live outside the womb) and without the amniotic fluid, his chances of developing into a normal healthy, baby were very low. Even if he survived, she was told that he would have many health challenges including an underdeveloped brain and fused limbs. They further told her that she was also putting herself at risk because infection would set in which can cause her not to conceive again. My heart was broken for them. I thought about the unfairness of the situation. How can this be possible? God, this seems like too much for them to bear! Little did I know, that God was in the details.

For many people, pregnancy and child-rearing is a normal part of life and it is. However, for many women and couples, what should be 'normal' in many cases turns out not to be so. Suzanna was 38 and that age group is called advanced maternal age, formally

.5

the geriatric age for pregnancy.

AdvanceFertility.com (Advance Fertility Center of Chicago) gave the following breakdown of percentage miscarriage by maternal age

Maternal age	Pregnancy loss rate
< 30	8%
30-34	12%
35-37	16%
38-39	22%

The American College of Obstetricians and Gynaecologists (ACOG) estimates that 26% of all pregnancies end in miscarriage and between 10-15% of those pregnancies end in miscarriages in the first trimester and 1 – 5% between 13 and 19 weeks. My daughter was 17 weeks pregnant and based on these statistics the fetus had a 2% chance of surviving.

I believe one of the hardest decisions a woman can make is to terminate a pregnancy, be it for health or other personal reasons. The day my daughter went to the emergency centre, the doctor told her that once the sac ruptured, she would go into labour within forty-eight hours. They believed that it was important that she fully understood the risk of possible infection setting in if she didn't terminate. Zack and Suzie discussed the situation and decided the following day that they would do nothing. If she went into labour it would be out of their hands. They decided to wait. That was the Thursday evening.

They waited for three days, until the following Monday and nothing happened as she did not go into labour. They revisited the doctor to check if the baby was still alive and to their amazement, he was not only alive, but his heartbeat was stronger than the previous three days. They were in a real conundrum because they did not want to terminate the pregnancy as the baby was clearly alive, however, based on the doctor's report they did not want to carry a baby to full-term, that had mental or physical challenges. They knew that many people with special needs live productive lives but they also knew that in some cases the disabilities were so grave that living a productive life was extremely challenging. The questions were, did they have the faith to trust God that their precious baby boy would survive? What mental and physical states would he be in if he survived?

As I mentioned previously, Suzie and Zack chose Ozzy as a possible name for the baby and I was not too keen on that name. However, when they spelt it and gave me the meaning, I immediately thought, Yes, this is a lovely name. Ozzy means 'divine power' and 'divine protector' another meaning is God's strong arrow. As someone who believes in the power of 'God's Word' when spoken in faith, I eventually became excited about the name Ozzy and began to like it. I also developed other reasons for liking the name Ozzy.

Zack and Suzanna's story is not an ordinary boy meets girl story. They met almost four years before on a flight on their way to California. Based on Suzie's description of Zack and her mental state of mind at that time I had some concerns. All parents have an idea of the person they would like their daughters and sons to marry and my first thought was that Zack did not fit the image I had. I thought that this was the last person I would choose for my only daughter to marry.

People look at the outward appearance, but God looks at the heart. (1 Samuel 16:7)

I was judging based on what my mind could comprehend but thanks be to God, He sees beyond what is on the outside. My concerns led me to speak with a very dear woman of God who offered to pray with me. We met a few times for about two months and prayed about the situation. After one particular prayer date when we were finished praying, she said, "I keep seeing Zack and Suzie as arrows in God's hand." That was two years before they were married. Remember one of the meanings of Ozzy's name is God's strong arrow.

Isaiah 49:2 NIV *"He made my mouth like a sharpened sword, in the shadow of his hand he hid me; he made me into a polished arrow and concealed me in his quiver."*

At that time, I didn't realise the power of these words from God spoken by my friend.

Mommy I Am Alive

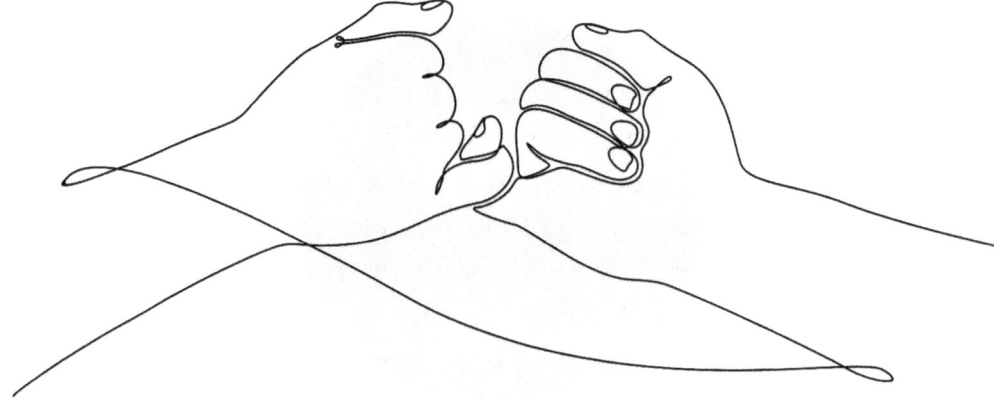

.9

Chapter 2

The Big Decision

Both Zack and Suzie are believers in Christ and their story shows the love of God in a very powerful way but that's not my story. It's theirs to tell at another time. After they went to visit the doctor and realised that the baby was still very much alive with a strong heartbeat, Zack and Suzie decided that they would not terminate the pregnancy. When faced with life-changing situations it helps when family members and loved ones are of the same mind. Fortunately for Zack and Suzie, their parents are believers in a God who can do miracles. Hence once they were not lacking in family support, they made the decision that they would trust God for the baby's daily provision of amniotic fluid, even though the doctors kept saying there was none.

We believed that if God could miraculously feed the people of Israel for forty years (Exodus 16:35) in the wilderness and if He could send a raven to feed a prophet, provide water from a dried-up brook and provide a widow with enough food to share her 'last meal' with the prophet and then multiply it to feed him, the widow and her son for three years (1 Kings 17:2-16) then providing amniotic fluid for a baby to grow and develop was no big deal. Zack and Suzie believed that God would preserve their precious baby boy and that he would be normal and healthy.

1 Corinthians 1: 18 -19, *"For the message of the cross is foolishness to those who are perishing, but to us who are being saved, it is the power of God. For it is written: 'I will destroy the wisdom of the wise; the intelligence of the intelligent I will frustrate.'"*

Some people believe that prayer is a mystery, while others believe that God will do what He wants to do so why bother to pray? The Scriptures said that Elijah the prophet, was a man like us and he prayed that it would not rain and for three and a half years and it did not rain (James 5:17). I believe that prayer may be a mystery and God is Sovereign but God wants us to pray. He wants us to come to Him in prayer for our needs. It is my deep belief that God our Heavenly Father, is pleased when we bring our petitions before Him. It shows a dependency on Him. One of the things about praying for a miracle is to be clear about what God is saying in the situation and to pray according to His good and perfect will. One can only get that clarity if one is having an intimate relationship with God. James chapter four speaks about drawing close to God and He will draw close to you. We do this by daily prayer, Bible reading and fellowship with God. Standing in faith means holding God to His promises. When we stand in faith, we need to find that portion of Scripture that speaks directly to our situation, that is called a Rhema word and hold God to His promises. The Spirit of God led me to the book of Mark and I found there my Rhema word that spoke directly to my present situation.

Mark 9:23, ESV: *"And Jesus said to him, "'If you can'! All things are possible for one who believes."*

This was my Rhema word. The Greek word Rhema means an exclamation. It signifies the action of an utterance, of coming alive. It is like the word became alive in my spirit. I, therefore, spoke the word daily because I believed that there is power in biblical utterances/ proclamations, speaking the word of God, out loud with boldness and confidence. I would pray, "Lord, your words say, … *'With man this is impossible, but with God all things are possible.'* " Matthew 19:26 NIV "Therefore, I believe all things are possible with You, I believe Ozzy is well!"

I am certain persons faced with similar situations, who decided to carry a pregnancy against their doctor's advice, may be criticised for being unwise. Some people may even wonder aloud, why would loving parents decide to keep a baby against the advice of medical professionals and take the chance of bringing a baby with potential medical issues into the world? They may even argue, that loving parents would not want to take the risk and bring a child into the world who may have mental or physical issues. The decision is a very difficult one and it comes down to personal choice.

As a family, we would love any baby that comes into our family. The fact is, we do have family members who are faced with raising a child with special needs and we know firsthand how difficult it is for everyone in the family. As we prayed for Ozzy, we prayed that he would have no major issues. However, we also acknowledged that God is sovereign and can take any situation and turn it around. Therefore our prayer also was, "Your will be done, Lord."

When Suzie and Zack shared with me their decision, I assured them that I would stand with them in prayer. We asked God to prepare us for whatever His will may be while praying for His supernatural intervention. I must confess that it was not always easy to stand in faith over the twelve weeks before Ozzy was delivered. However, I found another promise that came alive in my spirit.

Matthew 17:20-21 *"For truly I tell you, if you have faith the size of a mustard seed, you will say to this mountain, 'Move from here to there,' and it will move; and nothing will be impossible for you."*

These verses became my daily meal. I prayed them every morning and every evening for three months, reminding God of His promises.

Suzie's visits to the doctor were twice weekly and each time the news was the same; the baby's heartbeat was strong. However, without amniotic fluid, they could not tell what was happening. I must also mention that her primary doctor, a very compassionate woman was always encouraging. She gave them the facts but always reassured them that it was their choice. My daughter never once felt judged by this woman who also happened to be a believer in Christ.

In April, my sister went to California to give them practical support and she shared with me about one particular day when she took them to see the doctor. She said that after leaving the doctor's office, she looked at them and began to pray because they were so downcast as the report was always the same; the baby's heartbeat was strong but they could not see anything because of the lack of amniotic fluid. She said no word was spoken for the entire twenty-minute drive back to their house but she was silently praying.

For women like me who have had 'normal' pregnancies, we cannot understand the agony that women with difficult and high-risk pregnancies endure. I have two children and I admit that like most women I have never stopped to consider the process of the development of a baby. The fact is, the growth and development of a fetus is very defined with specific milestones at each stage. My daughter was just entering the second trimester which means that the baby's lung development had barely begun. Yes, he was a fully formed human being and his skeletal system was there and the organs including his heart were functioning as they should, but they were still very immature.

I believe as the Psalmist declared in Psalm 139:14 KJV *"… we are fearfully and wonderfully made."*

I believe that no matter the circumstance surrounding a baby's conception and birth, that child is fearfully and wonderfully made in the image and likeness of God. The Creator of the universe has placed in man His breath and with boldness I say, "Mankind is God's greatest creation." Having this thought gave us the strength to pray daily for Ozzy's survival and sustenance but it was all by faith as the doctors kept insisting that they could not see what was happening in the womb because there was no fluid for the ultrasound machine to read through.

I know that we all have faith in something. However, I know that people who may not understand the Christian faith can be challenged to give encouraging words in these kinds of situations. It may be felt by some that standing in faith is not a practical and wise decision. However, to those of us who believe that God can do what we cannot see, stand on His goodness and mercy. Hebrews 11:1 & 6 NIV says: *"Faith is confidence in what we hope for and assurance about what we do not see… And without faith it is impossible to please God because anyone who comes to him must believe that he exists and that he rewards those who earnestly seek him."*

Mommy I Am Alive

Chapter 3

The Consultation

Suzie works from home, however having made the decision not to terminate the pregnancy, she had to be on complete bed rest. I remember when I was pregnant with my son, I had to stop working at 36 weeks and be on bed rest and it was not a very pleasant experience. I cannot imagine what my daughter went through being on bed rest from 17 weeks pregnant until 29 weeks when she went into labour.

In those early days, it seemed that the amniotic fluid that we had prayed about, had miraculously come but as soon as she walked to the bathroom it leaked out. At one point I asked her, "If there was no fluid, how come there was leaking?" From that day onwards, our prayers were, "God continue to provide daily fluid for

Ozzy just like you provided daily manna for the children of Israel." A few days after we began praying that God would provide daily manna, Suzie had an interview with someone for a job as she is a talent acquisition manager. She called me after the interview and said "Mom, guess what's the name of the person I just interviewed? Manna!" This was taken as a sign from God that He was indeed providing manna for our Ozzy, and it built our faith to press into God. At this time we began to reach out to Christians all across the world to stand with us in prayer. One of the things that struck me was that not one person was negative. They all assured us that they would stand with us and they did. I would receive weekly calls from individuals reassuring me that they were praying and that God was in control. So I began journalling my reflective times with the Lord and the words that I received.

April 22, 2022 - My Prayer Journal

"Today, I thank you Lord for my unborn grandson who is fighting for his life in the womb. I thank you that he is healthy and strong and perfect physically, mentally and spiritually. I thank you that he will continue to grow and strive until the right time for delivery. Amen!"

The Consultation

At about 20 weeks gestation, Suzanna was referred to a doctor at The University of California Los Angeles (UCLA) hospital. At that consultation, she was told that if the pregnancy made it to 24 weeks, they would take her case and work with her, while reminding her of the negative consequences if the baby survived. She was told that he was much smaller than his gestational age and that in itself was a risk. The doctor explained to her all the things they would need to do. She was told that she would be given steroids to help develop the baby's lungs but there was no guarantee since they could not tell what was happening and if he even had lung tissue. She would also be given several injections to prevent infection from setting in and if all went according to plan, she would be in the hospital for 10 weeks. Suzie shared with me that she felt that not one of the doctors believed that she would make it to the 24 weeks and even if the baby made it, he would have many challenges. There were many days that she called me and cried because the science of the situation was so negative. The fact is, doctors are scientists, however, God is God and what He has ordained no man can reverse.

Isaiah 14:27 *"For the LORD Almighty has purposed, and who can thwart Him? His hand is stretched out, and who can turn it back?"*

With each passing day, we felt that God was in the midst of the situation and during the time of waiting for her to reach 24 weeks, she was encouraged by many mothers who had had similar experiences and had delivered healthy babies. This period was a very difficult time for the family since Suzie could literally, do nothing except stay in bed and continue to work from her bed. We were so blessed to have my sister staying with them and giving much-needed assistance for a few weeks. Little Finn could not understand why Mommy could not take him to the park or play with him anymore.

The day before she left for UCLA to check in, she called me and was very distressed just thinking about being in the hospital for 10 weeks. She shared with me her anxieties and uncertainties that were challenging her faith in God. I reassured her that God is faithful and He is a miracle worker and that we were praying for a miracle because technically a baby cannot survive without amniotic fluid for any length of time. Ozzy had made it to 24 weeks and we viewed this as a miracle so we continued to pray and praise God and thank Him for what He was doing.

James 5:16b *"The prayer of a person living right with God is something powerful to be reckoned with."* The Message Bible

The Consultation

22.

Mommy I Am Alive

Chapter 4

Five Long Weeks In The Hospital

It is said that no matter how difficult the task, it must begin with a single step. When the time came for Suzie to be admitted to the hospital for a moment my heart was in despair. I wanted to go to California and I could hear it in her voice that she wanted me to be there and accompany her. However, wisdom dictated that it was better for me to visit with her after the baby was delivered since she would need the help at that time. I promised her that I would be with her a week before the scheduled delivery.

To spend ten weeks in a hospital no matter how comfortable it may be could not be easy and I prayed with her that last night at home that all would be well on the two-hour drive to Los Angeles.

Thankfully, her in-laws were there with her and this made a big difference. That night I began a journal called, Ozzy and Suzie's Journey, and I began to count down.

May 27, 2022 - My Prayer Journal

Day 1 - Suzie's Journey in the Hospital

Ozzy shall live!

"Jesus said, "If there are no 'ifs' among believers. Anything can happen?." Mark 9:23 MSG

Father, I believe that with You all things are possible.

She was checked in and given all the necessary instructions. Here began a journey of five long weeks, a journey that had many highs and lows with mostly lows.

The psalmist says in Psalm 142: 11-2 MSG *"I cry out*

loudly to God, loudly I plead with God for mercy. I shout all my complaints before him, and spell out my troubles in detail."

For five long weeks, we had been literally, crying out to God for mercy, grace and for the life of our precious baby boy. Now at twenty-two weeks, there was still some ways to go. The doctors hoped for another ten weeks before delivery. I prayed to God for His timing because He is always on time and His time is perfect.

I think that the first night in the hospital must have been the most difficult one for Zack and Suzie. Zack stayed with her that first night to get her settled, then he had to leave the following day to take care of five-year-old Finn who was still in school.

Walking into the unknown with uncertainty is a very difficult thing to do. It was into the unknown because we just didn't know what was happening inside Suzie's tummy. All we had was our faith and belief in a God who is more than able, therefore we continued to trust and pray without ceasing that we were praying according to the will of God.

The Scriptures say in Hebrews chapter 11:1ESV *"Now faith is the assurance of things hoped for, the conviction of things not seen."*

The book of Hebrews outlines ordinary people who did extraordinary things because of their faith in God. The Scriptures have a lot to say about faith and as I said before, the scripture that lived with me throughout these months was Matthew 17:2 KJV I prayed, "Lord you said in your word that if I have faith as a grain of mustard seed I can remove mountains. I know that my faith is bigger than a mustard seed, therefore I have prayed expecting the desired outcome. I believed more than any other time that our faith is being tested as a family. I know for sure that mine has never been tested like this before."

During my many years on this journey as a believer, I have had many moments when I had to trust in God and hold on to His promises but never before in this way. One of my favourite quotes is by Oswald Chambers, that great Bible teacher in the 1800s, who penned in the book, *My Utmost for His Highest*:

"The height of the mountaintop is measured by the dismal drudgery of the valley, but it is in the valley that we have to live for the glory. We see His glory on the mountain, but we never live for His glory there. 'it's in the valley of despair that we see his glory."

There is more truth in these words than I realised before. Many believers, myself included, like to always have the mountain top experiences. It's natural, however, the reality is that it is not possible to live on the mountaintop permanently. God shows up in the valley of despair. It's in the darkest moments of life that we are able to see the hand of God at work.

The weeks and months of waiting certainly felt like we were walking in the valley without knowing where we were heading. However, with hope in our hearts and standing strong in faith, we were expectant, because we knew who we served, and we believed that nothing was impossible for Him to do.

Mommy I Am Alive

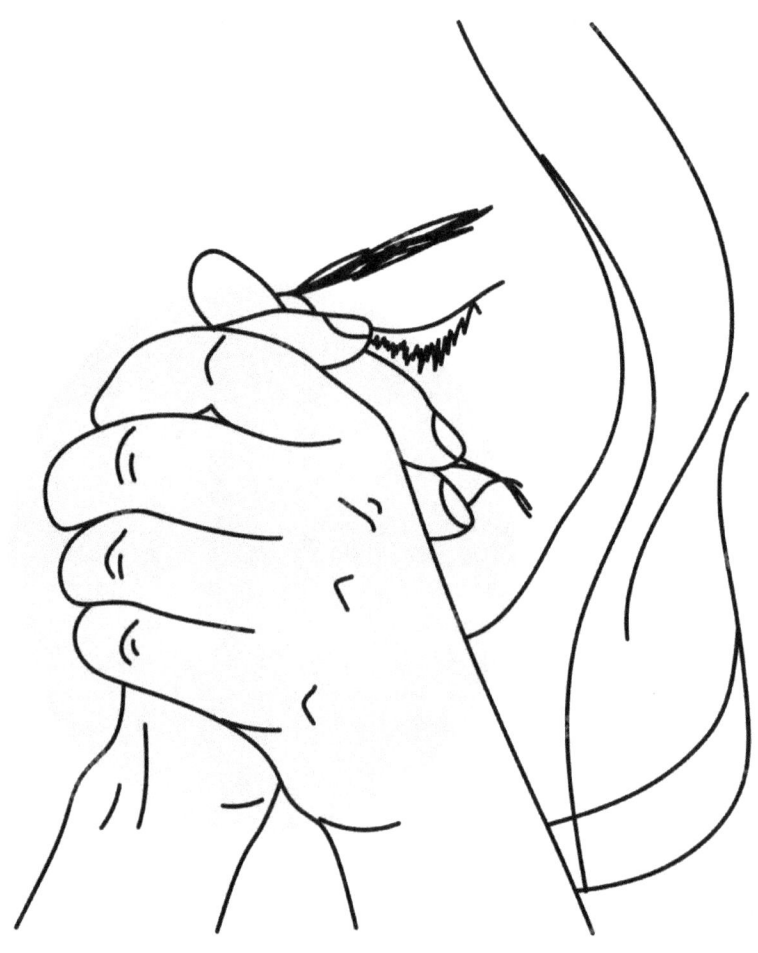

Chapter 5

Prayer and More Prayer

Suzie and I developed a kind of daily routine. We spoke early mornings, 4 am her time, 7 am my time. Usually, the nurses would go into her room to take her vitals at that time. She was not a happy camper during those early morning hours. However, in typical Suzie style, she soon developed relationships with nurses and doctors, alike. We also spoke during the days and in the evenings before I retired to bed. I called her and prayed and sometimes I would talk to Ozzy, all the while counting off the days.

There were many mornings that Suzie called and cried because the medical team had visited her and the not-very encouraging report was always the same; "Prepare yourself because we don't know what is happening."

One morning in particular, she called me, and she was crying because the news was very discouraging. The baby's weight was an issue as he was not putting on the required amount of weight for his gestational age. The doctors could not see the baby since there was no fluid in the sac, therefore they could not say what was happening. She was told that his stomach may be caved in, and he was still so tiny and underdeveloped at that time. Since the doctors could not see inside the amniotic sac and based on their scientific analysis and considering the statistics, she was told again, that the baby would have many challenges.

And so, I prayed…

June 21, 2022 - My Prayer Journal

Day 26 - Suzie's Journey in the Hospital

"Dear Lord, today the doctors gave Suzie further discouraging news, but we believe in your report that says Ozzy shall live. We believe your word that says if we believe all things are possible, they are. I draw upon Matthew 9:23 and Mathew 17:20. I trust that you are a kind and compassionate God. I also believe that you are a God of purpose.

Please show your purpose in this situation and may you be glorified, Amen!"

That night I prayed before I went to bed "Lord we need a sign, let it be that the next time that Ozzy is weighed, he will be at least two pounds." The following week she called and lo and behold, he weighed precisely two pounds. What a wonderful God!

"If you abide in Me, and My words abide in you, you will ask what you desire, and it shall be done for you" John 15:7 NKJV

If you ask any swimmer how difficult it is to swim upstream, they will share the ache in their tense and engaged muscles. Even with their powerful strokes, the water is relentless as their muscles push against it. Sometimes standing in faith is like swimming upstream. Many times, the currents that are pushing back are those of expert opinions. If possible, it can wear you down but faith is hard to die when you believe in a God that you have proven many times.

As the weeks went by, Suzie and I, with many believers across the world, continued to push against the tides in prayer.

We would always end the nights saying, "We believe the report of the Lord." and we thank God that He heard our hearts' cry. So, the routine continued until July 2, 2022.

Mommy I Am Alive

.33

Chapter 6

Labour of Love

So it was, after five weeks in the hospital, that Suzie went into labour and an emergency Caesarean section had to be done on July 2, 2022.

After retrieving my bag, I eventually got a flight to Los Angeles. Zack called at about the same time and said the baby and mother were well. The baby was breathing and cried when they took him out! To say my heart was full of gratitude is putting it mildly. I cried, I laughed, I cried again and began to laugh. I knew that the fact that he was breathing was a big deal, however, I didn't know anything else but it didn't matter as he was alive and breathing. I was also aware that the journey for us had only just begun.

During the long flight to LA, I kept praying that all was well. I was so consumed with a sense of relief that I sat beside a man who was very rude to me but it didn't matter. Even when a couple seated across the aisle heard his racist remarks and apologised, offering me a seat beside them, I didn't care. My grandson was alive and my daughter was well, that was all that mattered.

I sat on that plane and for the entire six hours, I silently prayed. I recalled the past months and I gave God thanks. I could not wait to see my grandson and in my heart, I believed and trusted God that all was well.

July 2, 2022 - Prayer Journal

Day 1 - Ozzy is born!

I reflected on the scripture in Luke 8:43-48:

"Now there was a woman who had been suffering from haemorrhages for twelve years; and though she had spent all she had on physicians, no one could cure her. She came up behind Jesus and touched the fringe of his clothes, and immediately her haemorrhage stopped." NRSVA

This woman had the faith that, since the doctors could not help, she turned to the One who she believed could help her. I know that the prayers of many people for Ozzy had been heard by God. I believe that God looks at our faith and He looks deep within our innermost being and sees the total submission and reliance upon Him. God meets us at the point of our needs. He saw that our faith was certain that He could do more than we could ask or imagine (Ephesians 3:20-21).

Praying takes the believer into another realm of the unknown and unseen, it causes us to rely on a spiritual person who is much bigger than us, this is the spiritual realm. The Scripture says that those who come to God must come in Spirit and Truth. We cannot see but we are confident that He exists and He is a rewarder of those who diligently seek Him.

Psychiatrists say that prayer is therapeutic and encourage people who may be depressed to meditate and pray. For me, prayer is saying to my Maker, my God, "I cannot do this but I know You can."

The psalmist David, said in Psalm 46:1 *"God is a present help in the time of need."* KJV

Mommy I Am Alive

.37

Chapter 7

Trusting And Giving Thanks

The night of July 2, 2022, at approximately 9:30 pm, my son-in-law met me at the Los Angeles airport. His face was full of life, his entire face was smiling, eyes beaming with joy. I remember thinking, *this kind of joy cannot be purchased with money.* It's a joy that is pure and it's full of gratitude to God for life. I must have stepped on a bus and I must have seen many people but the only thing that I was cognisant of was Zack sitting beside me and we never said another word to each other on the way to the hospital, we were just content to be precisely where we were.

I entered my daughter's room at the University of California, Los Angeles (UCLA) hospital. It was very emotional! I saw her in the bed and I whispered a prayer of thanksgiving because even though I was standing in faith, there were moments of wondering how she would get through this. The room was the usual hospital room, clean smell, white walls and small with limited space. She was half asleep on her back and sleepily opened her eyes when I walked in. There was a sofa against the wall and a chair beside the bed. The room seemed comfortable and, having been there for five weeks, she had made it her home away from home. Pictures of her family were on the walls and special personal items that made the room more friendly and less sterile were on a shelf.

We spoke and then I asked to visit the baby even though it was way past 10 p.m. I found the staff to be friendly and very accommodating. In moments like these, it is so important to have good hospital staff support. I visited the hospital several times per day over a one-month period and I never had a bad encounter. All the nurses and doctors were very professional, understanding and accommodating.

When I stepped into the Neonatal Unit that night, the place was very quiet. It seemed that all the babies were asleep. There was a sense of peace and stillness as if all was well. No one would have thought that babies were fighting for their lives and parents were quietly praying by their sides. The lights were low and the nurses were sitting at their station quietly working. One of them looked up when I entered and asked if I was Ozzy's grandmother. She showed me his unit and I looked and saw the tiniest little human I had ever seen. He was hooked up to what appeared to be a crib, except that it had all kinds of machines monitoring his vitals, his temperature and it seemed his entire body. My heart was so full of gratitude that the fact he weighed only two pounds and was on a ventilator made little difference to me. I knew there and then that I was looking at a miracle and that the God I serve had heard our prayers and delivered Ozzy safely to us, as I knew He would. I also knew that Ozzy would be okay and that he would live to tell his story for generations to come.

There is a song I used to listen to every morning on my way to work. The title is, "The story I will tell." Yes, I thought, Ozzy, will indeed tell his story one of these days.

In the days and weeks that followed, I saw one miracle after the other. Suzie was discharged after three days even though she was very reluctant to leave. The reality was that the doctors were still on guard and even after two weeks they were warning us not to be too optimistic because premature babies sometimes have honeymoon periods. However, our faith and trust in God never wavered. We knew that God had stepped in and Zack and Suzie were experiencing a miracle; all for the glory of God.

July 2, 2022 - Prayer Journal

Day 1 - (2ⁿᵈ entry) Thank the Lord for Ozzy!

Lord, what can I say, except thank you? Ozzy is alive and well, delivered today. He came out with a fist in the air and crying. What a mighty God you are? When man said no, you said not so! Hallelujah! You are a miracle-working miracle God. You watch over your promises to bring them to pass. You said if we have faith like a grain of mustard seed we can move mountains. Yes Lord, we trust you, you are a mighty God, Amen!

July 3, 2022 - Prayer Journal

Day 2 - Lord, keep helping Ozzy and Suzie

Lord how can I say thanks for what you have done? By your Spirit you have done a great miracle and I give you all the praise. Father may you continue to do what you have started. I lift up

Ozzy's lungs, I thank you for closing those air pockets. I thank you for his stability, may he continue to grow and put on weight in the coming weeks. I pray that Suzie's milk will come in so that he will be able to get his mother's milk. You are truly amazing, a promise keeper, a way maker and I love you Lord and trust you, Amen.

Mommy I Am Alive

Chapter 8

Miracles Do Happen

As I stated earlier, I saw one miracle after the other during the four weeks that I stayed with Suzie and Zack. God provided accommodation operated by the hospital that was not very expensive, less than ten minutes from the hospital. Initially, we had the money for one month, we were so grateful when God provided the money to pay for the hotel accommodation for two months. This was such a blessing because Ozzy could not leave UCLA hospital until the doctors were comfortable that he could swallow and breathe at the same time. Suzie had to stay close to the hospital as she had to pump and take milk for the baby. Finn and Zack could also stay since it was summer break. This was good as both parents took turns visiting Ozzy while I stayed with Finn.

Thankfully, the situation was a mixed blessing as I was able to spend precious time with Finn. During those four weeks that I was there with them it was great, as I was able to take Finn to the park and have special times with him. It was a delight as together we visited a few playgrounds and even got lost on one of our trips. He could not understand why his mommy and baby brother could not go home with him and our times together were a timely distraction.

During these weeks I observed a tiny little human who wanted not only to live but also for others to see that he was here. The nurses were quite enamoured with him, and he was very alert, even recognising when a particular nurse was with him. He was so alert that one day I asked if he could see me, as his tiny face was looking up intently into mine. At two weeks old he turned his little head and looked in my direction as soon as he heard my voice. The nurse told me that he couldn't make out forms but he was aware of people around him and knew voices. We began to hold him at two weeks, and he would at times look intently into our faces as if he was trying his hardest to see what we looked like.

I also saw my daughter's strength in those early days, as I know that it must have been very difficult and very emotional at times. Sometimes after leaving the hospital, she would sit quietly and cry and other times she stayed at the hospital until very late at night. I became concerned for her health, as her feet became swollen and her blood pressure was high.

One night when Suzie came back from the hospital, I knew something was not right, her demeanour was one of discouragement and despondency, and she was very downcast. She said that while she was there, Ozzy had an episode of desaturating. This is when babies in NICU oxygen levels go below the normal range for breathing and their heart rate gets really low. She said it was very scary as he was not responding for a few seconds. We were told to expect more episodes like these but we continued to give God thanks as we knew that for each crisis there would be a miracle that followed.

Zack, the nurses and I tried to encourage Suzie to go home to Santa Barbara for a day and night but she was very reluctant. Eventually, one of the nurses **CONVINCED HER** to go home and start preparing for Ozzy to be home. I believe this was what she needed to hear. Therefore, when Ozzy was three weeks old we went to Santa Barbara for a day and spent the night. Of course, Suzie called every hour, thankfully the nurses understood.

Ozzy became so popular that a nurse told me that I had a 'Rock Star' for a grandson as she noticed that some of the other nurses from different areas wanted to see him.

At two months, Ozzy was transferred to the hospital in Santa Barbara as the doctors were now confident that he had passed the worst. This new arrangement was much easier on the family since they lived just a few minutes from the hospital.

When Ozzy was transferred to Cottage Hospital in Santa Barbara, Suzie gave us access to view him on the monitor from home. This was such a special time because we got to know his little personality. He was certainly a demanding little man. He was a very engaging, premature baby and the nurses were quite taken by him. I admit that many nights I called Suzie (from Jamaica) and told her Ozzy was crying and she needed to call the hospital and find out what was the matter! I guess Mothers are just like that after all.

○ ○ ○ ○ ○ ○ ○ ○ ○

July 6, 2022 - Prayer Journal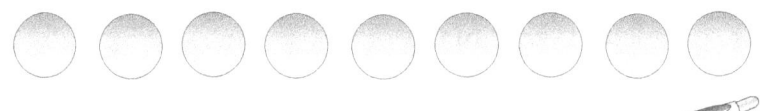

Day 5 - Ozzy and Suzie's Journey

Father there is so much to thank you for, my grandson Ozzy is doing more than I could ask or imagine. You have done what doctors said could not be done. Ozzy is perfect, he is so precious, you have silenced the critics and you have done very well. Thank you God, my Father, my Creator. Thank you that you are a promise keeper, you said that if I believe, all things are possible. Ozzy is the result and I praise you, all glory and praise is yours, all glory and worship go to you, Amen.

●●●●●●●●●

July 9, 2022 - Prayer Journal

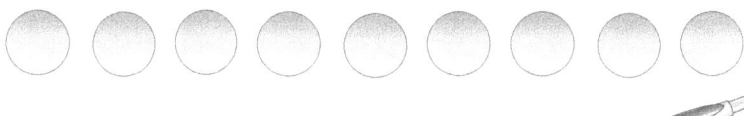

Day 8 - Ozzy and Suzie's Journey

Ozzy is one full week today. Dear God how can I thank you enough? Last evening I visited and he looked straight at me and smiled. I know that doctors say that babies this young cannot smile but I know that it was a smile, this little miracle is so alert! I pray against any lung disease, I pray that he will not be on oxygen for too long. Oh Lord my God, thank you, thank you, Amen!

Mommy I Am Alive

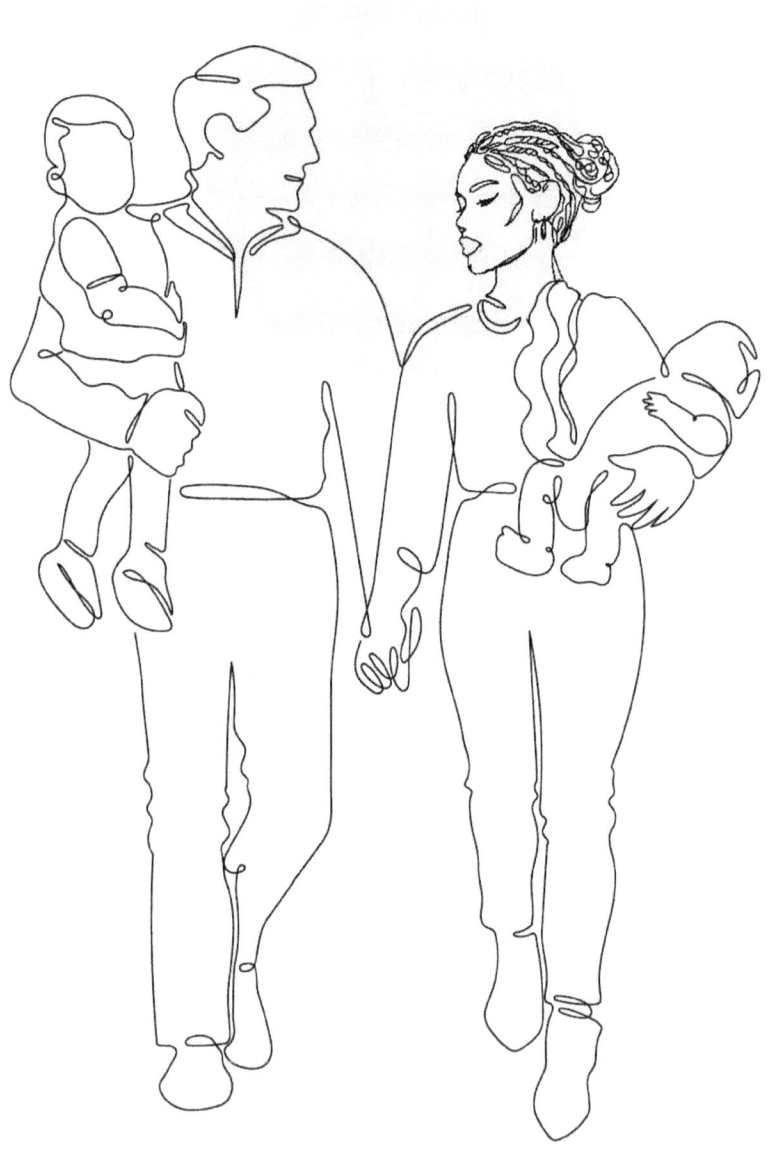

.49

Chapter 9

To God Be The Glory!

After three months in the NICU, Ozzy graduated from the hospital. He went home with oxygen as his little lungs were still underdeveloped, but we knew that God's hand was still at work. Ozzy went home in September and was taken off oxygen in December. Notwithstanding, that we were cautioned that he would be on oxygen from at least age one and maybe beyond, our little miracle was doing just great.

The first few weeks for Zack and Suzie were not as difficult as they could have been. They were so happy to have their beautiful baby boy home that nothing could prevent them from being content. Their concern was ensuring that Ozzy's oxygen levels were good. Once he was at home there were no crises that caused concerns that sometimes happen. For example, there was no rushing him back to the hospital for treatment as often happens because 'preemies' go into crisis sometimes when they go home.

At eight months, Ozzy had been given the clear to travel as his lungs were now fully developed! He is bright and alert, and laughs and giggles a lot. His doctors are well pleased with him and how well he is doing.

I praise God without ceasing for the miracle of Ozzy, and like the Psalmist declared in Psalms 136:1-4.

"I Give thanks to the Lord, for He is good. His love endures forever. Give thanks to the God of gods. His love endures forever. Give thanks to the Lord of lords: His love endures forever. To Him who alone does great wonders, His love endures forever."
NIV

I will give thanks forever because God is the One, the only One who can decree, and no one can reverse it and His love endures forever.

Photo Album

Zack and Suzanna

The author and her daughter (Suzie)

The author and husband at Zack and Suzie's wedding

Zack and Suzie with Ozzy in an incubator at the hospital

Ozzy and parents finally going home from the hospital

Big brother Finn and Ozzy

Ozzy and Grandma Janice

Ozzy dresssed for his birthday

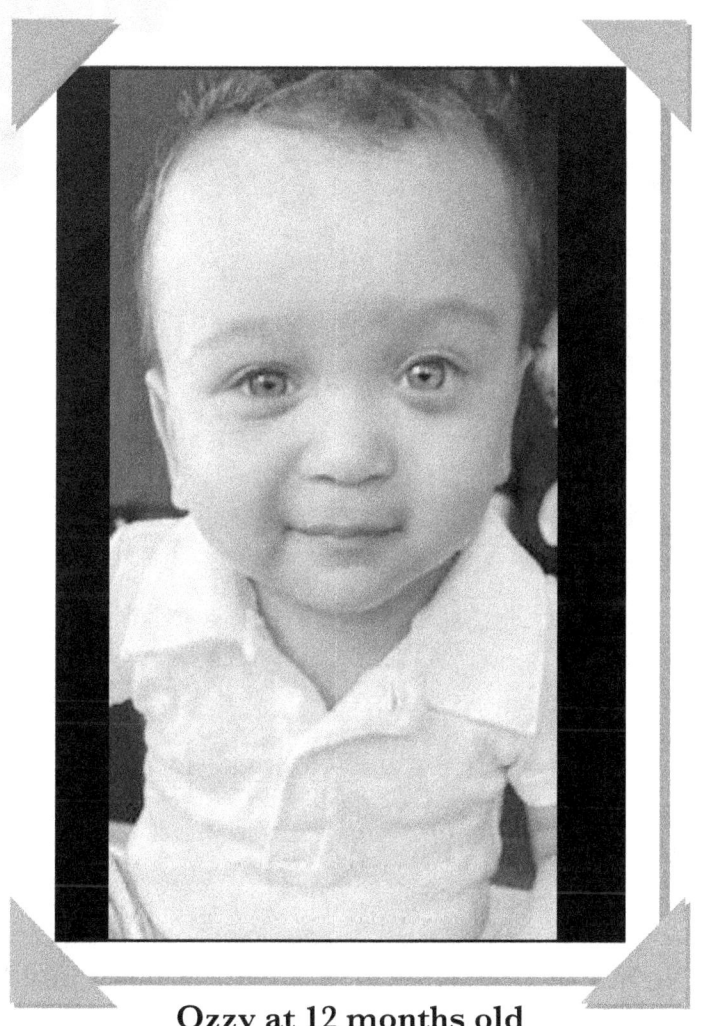

Ozzy at 12 months old

Mommy I Am Alive

The happy family - Zack, Suzanna, Finn and Ozzy

The miracle of baby Ozzy continues ...

About The Author

Janice A. Lee has worked in various senior positions in the private sector in her homeland Kingston, Jamaica.

She is a Christian of over forty years and is passionate about sharing her faith with others. She is a small group leader in her local church, a speaker and a published author having published her first book - **Rivers in the Dessert,** in 2013, she also has a YouTube Channel of the same name where she shares her faith while encouraging other believers.

Janice was educated at the University of the West Indies, Mona and holds a Masters in Business Administration, and a postgraduate certificate in Administration and Education. Janice is married to Michael Lee and has two adult children Suzanna and Mark and three grandchildren, Finn, Liam and Ozzy.

www.ingramcontent.com/pod-product-compliance
Lightning Source LLC
Chambersburg PA
CBHW071024080526
44587CB00015B/2491